Greetings shopkeepers, crafts people, and skilled or unskilled

I stand before you, like Horatius on/at/on/at the bridge, protecting the cultural currency of a traditional British education from Etruscan hoards, enemies of progress and constructivists alike.

Initially, my plan, much like Dionysius of Halicarnassus in producing his 'Rhōmaikē Archaiologia', was to produce a moral document, through which I might continue the Herculean task of enriching the intellectual life of the working classes, much as an autodidact manual worker might have done, himself, in better times when the poor were properly deserving of our patronage. Previously, I have gifted each school the King James' Bible (onto the spine of which I dutifully transcribed my own position, as inspiration and chief begetter); yet I was accused of being as hubristic as Midias, when first assaulting Demosthenes.

And so, I offer to you, a curriculum aid for intellectually straightened times: *The Michael Gove Colouring-in Book,* as inspired by me, Secretary of State for Education. In producing this I have drawn together a committee of the great and the good (and Carol Vorderman); all of whom have advised on its contents. You might use this either 'As You Like It', or, alternatively, do with it 'What You Will'. However, I have a number of suggestions that, acknowledging my position as Britain's foremost educationalist, you might want to consider.

You are, of course, now aware that children do not have special educational needs. There are some who, through their own fault, or through that of their feckless parents, are simply thick. You might want to use this, *the Michael Gove colouring-in book,* written by me, Secretary of State for Education, as a differentiated activity for those students who are never going to trouble sainted halls with effortless classical allusion. You might also consider it as an appropriate candidate for being, alongside Dryden and Pope, one of the fifty books per year that students should read. Alternatively, there are enough pictures of me, Michael Gove, Secretary of State for Education, to please anyone with a tutored interest in aesthetics: it is recommended that higher ability in the soon-to-be reinstated grammar schools are allowed twenty minutes of silent adoration during form period.

As an addendum, any business magnates interested in providing the £370,000 (or so) of sponsorship it will require to have this text sent to every school in the country can be assured that any desire to take over a range of functioning educational institutions, specifically to name those institutions after themselves, will be looked on, neither as mendacity, nor as an act of hubris as serious as Timarchas's when he submitted himself to prostitution and unnatural intercourse, but as an example of thriving democracy in action.

Keep saving up the money to attend classical concerts!

ENGLISH
Writing

co-lon 1
n. pl. co-lons
a. A punctuation mark (:) used after a word
introducing a quotation, explanation, example

co-lon 2
n. pl. co-lons or co-la
The section of the large intestine
extending from the cecum
to the rectum

COLOUR KEY

1 !
2 ?
3 /
4 <

PHONICS

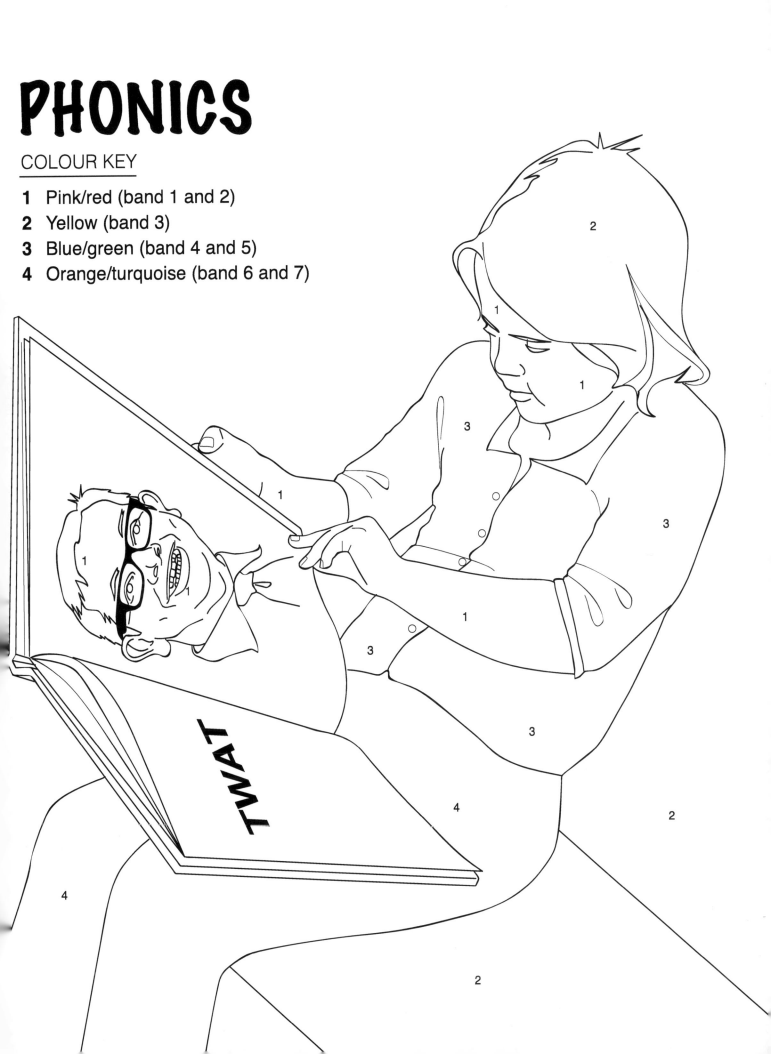

SPEAKING & LISTENING

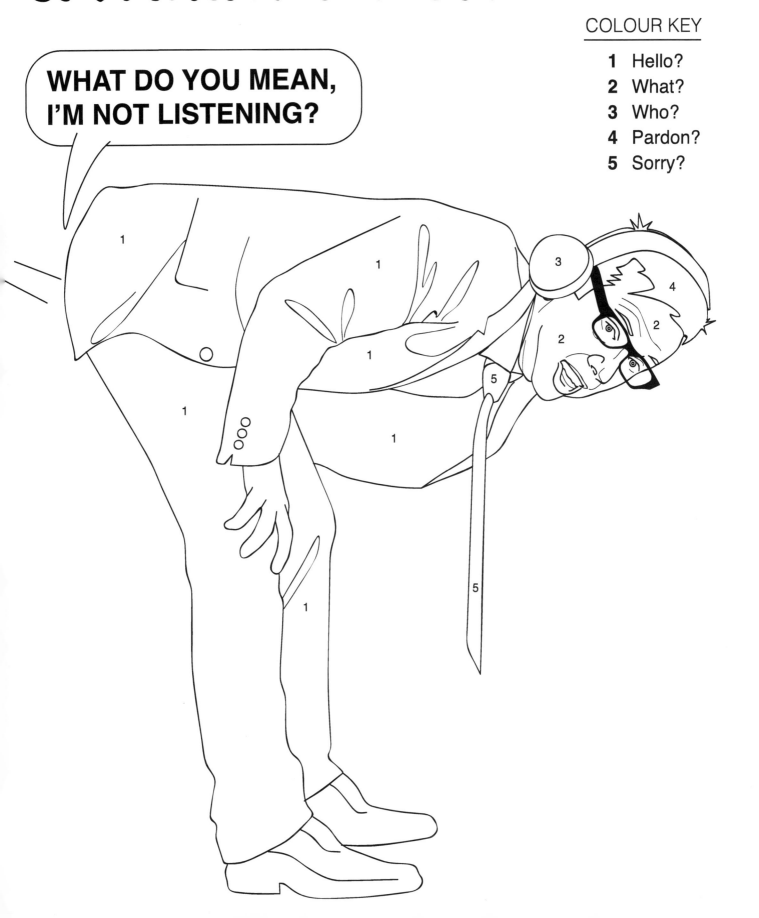

LATIN

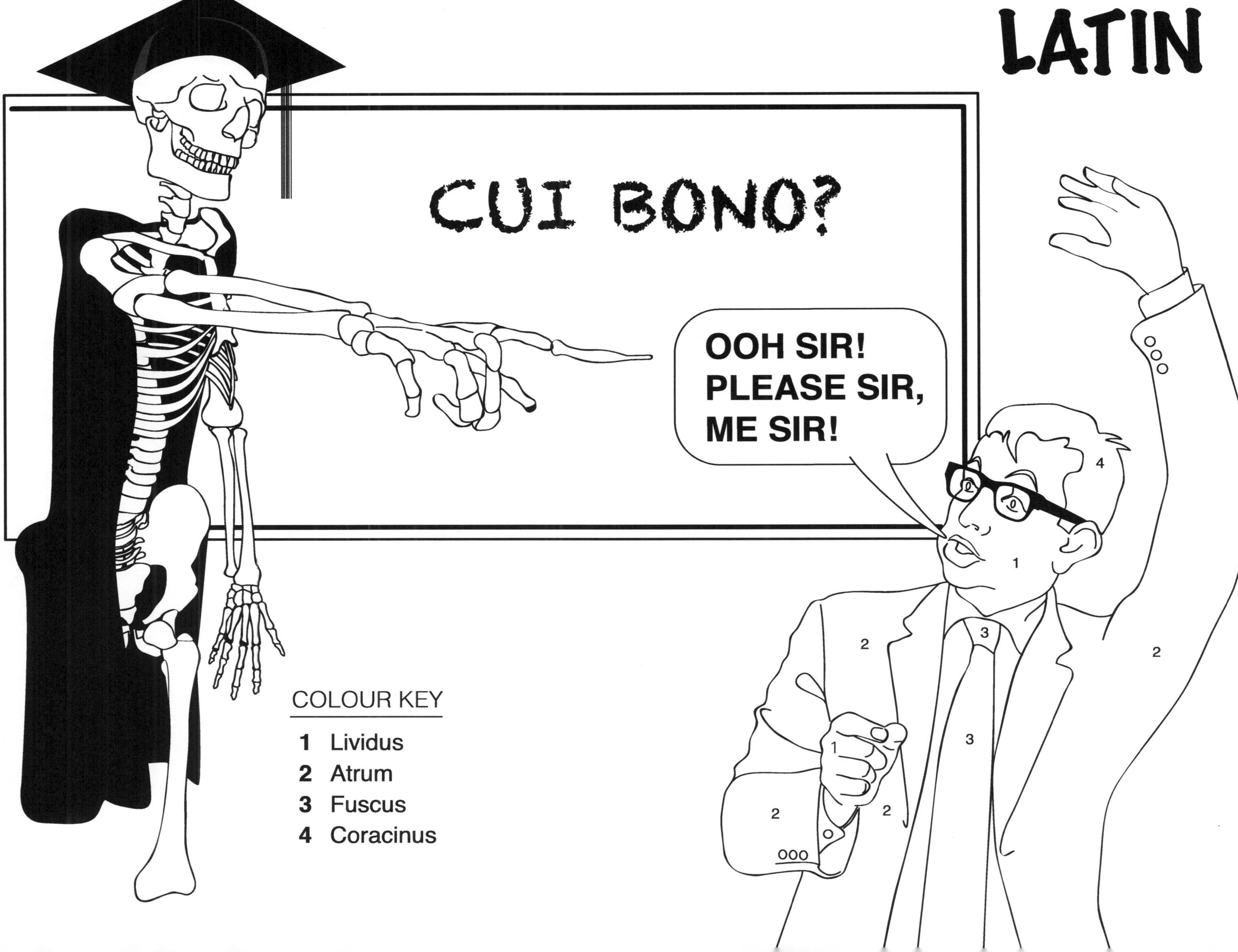

COLOUR KEY

1 Lividus
2 Atrum
3 Fuscus
4 Coracinus

SELF-KNOWLEDGE

COLOUR KEY

1 It's
2 Only
3 Skin
4 Deep

GEOGRAPHY/ HISTORY

COLOUR KEY

1 Red

2 White

3 Blue

4 Pink

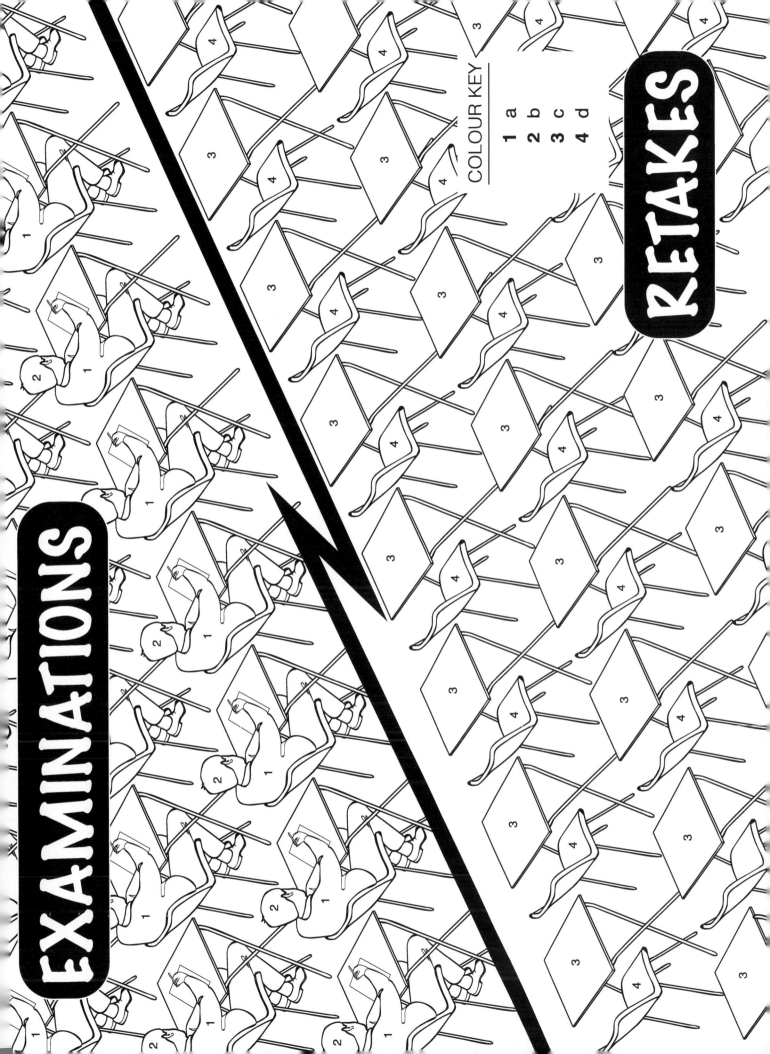

ART

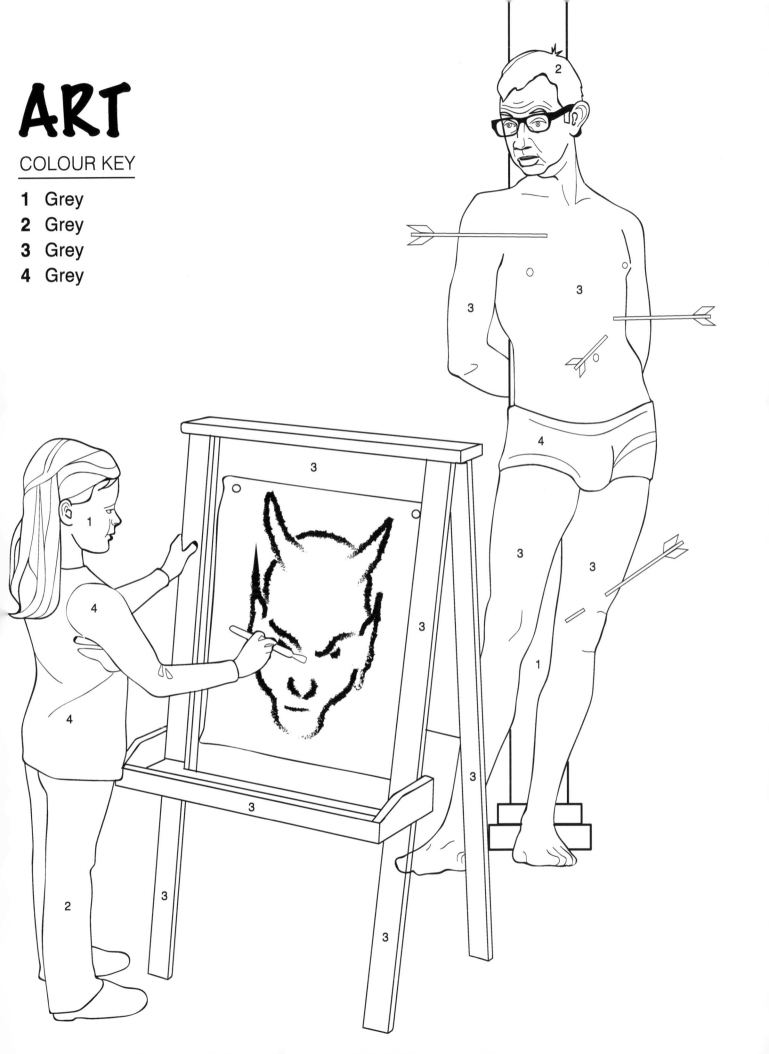

FOOD TECHNOLOGY

COLOUR KEY

1 Done
2 Overdone
3 Burnt
4 Buggered

SOFT SUBJECTS

Sociology

Banned knowledge for
working class children

Theatre studies

Banned knowledge for
working class children

Media studies

Banned knowledge for
working class children

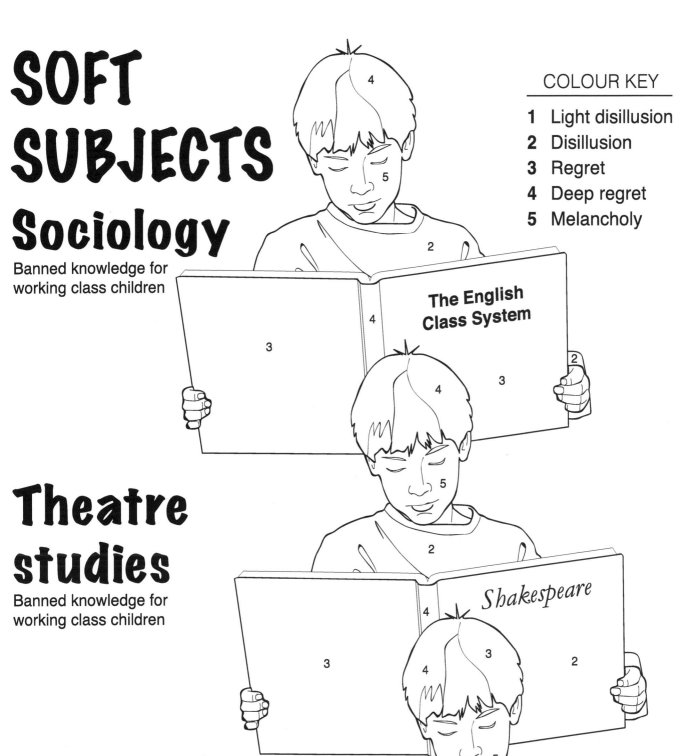

The English
Class System

Shakespeare

THE Sun

Keeping you stupid
for the last 50 years

National Curriculum Vitae

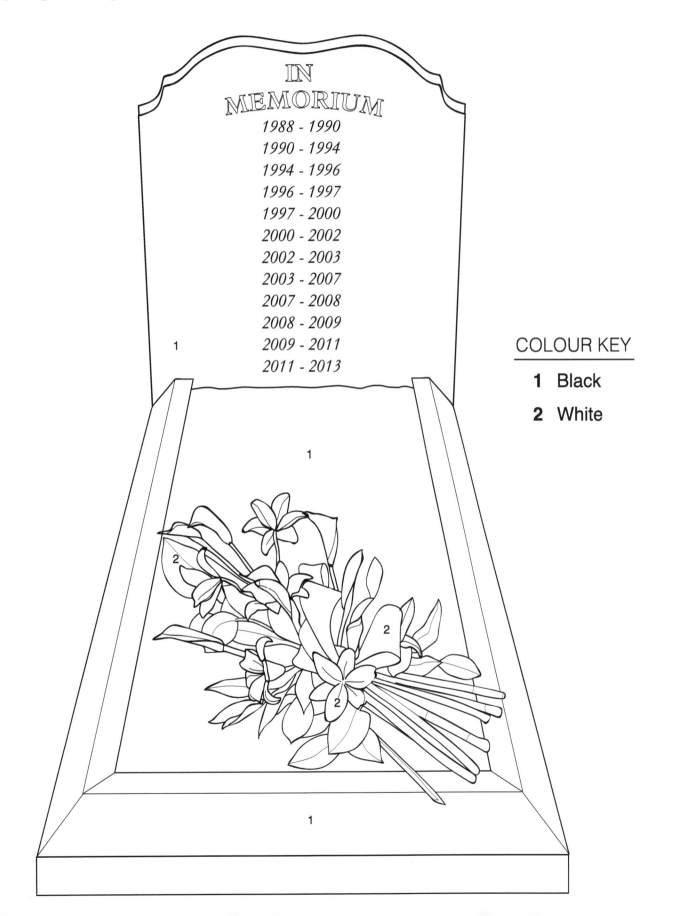

IN
MEMORIUM

1988 - 1990

1990 - 1994

1994 - 1996

1996 - 1997

1997 - 2000

2000 - 2002

2002 - 2003

2003 - 2007

2007 - 2008

2008 - 2009

2009 - 2011

2011 - 2013

COLOUR KEY

1 Black

2 White

Printed in Great Britain
by Amazon.co.uk, Ltd.,
Marston Gate.